ALASDAIR MOR GRANT

From the portrait by R. Waitt at Castle Grant,
by permission of the Countess of Seafield.

PERSONAL ARMS OF LORD STRATHSPEY,
CHIEF OF CLAN GRANT

JOHNSTON'S CLAN HISTORIES

THE CLAN GRANT

Clansman's Badge

JOHNSTON'S CLAN HISTORIES

THE CLAN CAMERON. BY C.I. FRASER OF REELIG, *Sometime Albany Herald.*

THE CLAN CAMPBELL. BY ANDREW MCKERRAL, C.I.E.

THE CLAN DONALD. (Macdonald, Macdonell, Macalister). BY I.F. GRANT, LL.D.

THE FERGUSSONS.
BY SIR JAMES FERGUSSON OF KILKERRAN, BT.

THE CLAN FRASER OF LOVAT.
BY C.I. FRASER OF REELIG, *Sometime Albany Herald.*

THE CLAN GORDON. BY JEAN DUNLOP, PH.D.

THE GRAHAMS. BY JOHN STEWART OF ARDVORLICH.

THE CLAN GRANT. BY I.F. GRANT, LL.D.

THE KENNEDYS. BY SIR JAMES FERGUSSON OF KILKERRAN, BT.

THE CLAN MACGREGOR. BY W.R. KERMACK.

THE CLAN MACKAY. BY MARGARET O. MACDOUGALL.

THE CLAN MACKENZIE. BY JEAN DUNLOP, PH.D.

THE CLAN MACKINTOSH. BY JEAN DUNLOP, PH.D.

THE CLAN MACLEAN. BY JOHN MACKECHNIE.

THE CLAN MACLEOD. BY I.F. GRANT, LL.D.

THE CLAN MACRAE. BY DONALD MACRAE.

THE CLAN MORRISON. BY ALICK MORRISON.

THE CLAN MUNRO. BY C.I. FRASER OF REELIG, *Sometime Albany Herald.*

THE ROBERTSONS. BY SIR IAIN MONCREIFFE OF THAT ILK, BT. *Albany Herald.*

THE CLAN ROSS. BY DONALD MACKINNON, D.LITT.

THE SCOTTS. BY JEAN DUNLOP, PH.D.

THE STEWARTS. BY JOHN STEWART OF ARDVORLICH.

THE CLAN GRANT

THE DEVELOPMENT OF A CLAN

BY
I. F. GRANT, LL.D.
Author of: *The Lordship of the Isles, The Social and Economic Development of Scotland before 1603, Etc.*

With Tartans and Chief's Arms in Colour, and a Map

JOHNSTON & BACON PUBLISHERS
EDINBURGH AND LONDON

First published 1955
Reprinted 1969
Reprinted 1972

© *Johnston & Bacon Publishers*

SBN 7179 4526 X

PRINTED IN GREAT BRITAIN BY
LOWE AND BRYDONE (PRINTERS) LIMITED, LONDON

The Clan Grant

THE history of Clan Grant is less eventful than that of many clans. There are some exciting incidents—actual or traditional—but, on the whole, the chiefs steadily consolidated their fine patrimony and the clan continued to flourish. No Grant could wish the story to have been otherwise. The history of the Grants, however, is exceptionally interesting in its illustrations of how a clan was organised and therefore it seems best to write this brief account of the Grants from that angle.

Although branches of the clan have established themselves elsewhere, the Grants are especially associated with Strathspey and the thirty miles between the two Craigellachies—from Aviemore, where the river passes from the uplands of Badenoch, to where, its course almost run, it enters the coastal plain of Moray. The splendid river like its tributaries owes its peaty waters and tremendous pace to its origins in the high hills. Its winding course of amber-flecked shallows and pools of midnight darkness runs through a pleasant patchwork of fine arable land, diversified by dark masses of pine forests, where the ordered battalions of the plantings reinforce the branchy survivors of the ancient Caledonian Forest. Ramparts of heathery hills bound the Strath on either side, rising to the bleak ranges of the Monadhliath (Grey Hills) and the massive summits of the Monadh Ruadh (Cairngorms). About the whole Strath and its river there is a feeling of amplitude and dignity.

The other most considerable area acquired by the Chief and his kinsfolk is formed by the two adjoining Straths of Glenurquhart and Glenmoriston. They run parallel to each other into the wild country on the northern side of Loch Ness, not thirty miles from Strathspey as the crow or rather the eagle might fly over loch and hill, but, even for the feet of a Highlandman, they would be a march of some forty or fifty miles away. Glenurquhart has considerable stretches of good, arable land and flourishing woods cling to the winding contours of the slopes that bound it. Glenmoriston is bleaker and wilder and winds up into the great mass of high hills that form the centre of the Northern Highlands—a lonely land traversed by the tracks used of old by the hunters, the drovers and, above all, the reivers from Lochaber and Kintail. It was in the remotest fastnesses at the head of Glenmoriston that Prince Charles Edward was sheltered by the Seven Men of Glenmoriston when his pursuers had almost closed about him in the Hebrides.

There are several traditions about the origin of the Grants. There is a pleasant tale that the three crowns in the Coat of Arms were given to an ancestor named Hacken by the kings of the three Scandinavian kingdoms. There are more widely accepted though varying traditions that trace their descent from the ancient Gaelic Kings of Alba through the MacGregors. With the Gael kinship and kindness were closely associated, and the theory explains, or is explained by, the help the Grants gave to the MacGregors when they were proscribed. There is, however, documentary evidence strongly suggesting that the ancestor of the Grants was an Anglo-Norman, a member of the able and ambitious group who so largely re-shaped the social structure of Scotland.

Between the thirteenth and fifteenth centuries the names of about a dozen Grants are recorded in the North. The earliest is Sir Laurence le Grant, Sheriff of Inverness in 1263-64, who, according to tradition, was the son of Gregory the Great, said also to have been a Sheriff of Inverness. (In those lawless times only men powerful enough themselves to enforce the law were given the office of Sheriff.) Laurence's son, John, was certainly captured by the English in 1296 in Baliol's forlorn campaign against Edward I. According to tradition he later supported William Wallace and Andrew Moray in their heroic struggle. He acquired Inverallan in Strathspey in 1316, and the family also owned Stratherrick (a district to the south of Loch Ness), but it died out in the male line and with the marriage of the heiress the lands passed to other families.[1]

There were, however, other Grants, collaterals, in the North. We hear of two more members of the family fighting against the English. One of them and another Grant were men of affairs, receiving safe-conducts for important missions to France and England (one of these safe-conducts included his wife and ten servants). The son of this ambassador was probably the husband of Bigla, the heiress of Glencharnie.

Bigla, or Matilda, the ruins of whose castle still stand near Nethybridge, was according to tradition the daughter of a Comyn. After most sanguinary fighting with the Grants, he and his men are said to have taken refuge in a church. The pious Grants, to avoid the sacrilege of entering the church to slay them, set fire to it and burnt them to death instead. The leader of the Grants then married the heiress. Actually Bigla was the daughter of Gilbert, Lord of Glencharnie, a cadet of the Earls of Stratherne, and her lands were inherited by her son, Sir Duncan Grant. They consisted of Glencharnie (largely covered by the present parish of Duthil) and of half the

[1] Inverallan was later bought back by another branch of the family.

Barony of Freuchie. In a document of 1453 he was first styled " of Freuchie." His descendant built a castle there in 1536, which was afterwards called Bellachastle and Castle Grant. According to tradition Freuchie had been a Comyn stronghold. The son of the Chief of Grant, then in poor circumstances and much oppressed by the Comyns, had made a runaway match with the daughter of the Chief of the MacGregors who was extremely powerful. MacGregor pursued the young couple and found them sheltering in a cave near the castle of Freuchie, the lights of which could be seen from the cave's mouth. Taking pity on their poverty, the great Chief of the MacGregors captured Freuchie from the Comyns and gave it to them.

In reality it was not as simple as that. With the introduction of the feudal system Strathspey had been divided piecemeal among many landholders—local nobles, the Church, and Lowland families such as the Maynes, with whom Grant had a prolonged lawsuit, and others—and had been much broken up. The half Barony of Freuchie which Grant inherited consisted of two separate pieces. Many of the other lands bought by the family were even more scattered. Another complication was the vagueness of the titles by which much of the land was owned, which led to constant disputes. For instance, about 1482 the second Laird of Freuchie bought a claim to the ownership of Inverallan, but it took nearly two hundred years of litigation to obtain undisputed possession. In the case of Freuchie, which was in the Earldom of Moray, a yearly feu-duty was payable, and, as the Earldom was vacant, was paid to the King. In 1501, the Earldom was bestowed on the infant illegitimate son of James IV, and for seventeen years Grant paid the feu-duty to the administrator for the Earl. Then, James V having reached manhood and assumed control of his kingdom, Grant was threatened

GRANT

GRANT HUNTING TARTAN

with the forfeiture of his lands for having failed to pay the feu-duty to the King. In spite of a visit to Edinburgh, he had to pay up and failed to get compensation from the Earl of Moray.

There were about seven major purchases of land, most of them taking years to complete, as well as many small ones, in the building up of what by 1653 was described as " ane great hudge estait." Various charters consolidating the estate were secured from the King, the most important in 1694. In those lawless times no one could occupy land who could not defend it. Superiors chose vassals who could ensure the payment of rent by keeping out raiders and looking after their people. It was for this reason that the Grants were given occupation of so much Church land, and in 1509 James IV had bestowed Glenurquhart (which had become a lawless no-man's-land) upon John, second Laird of Freuchie, in order to secure " *policia* " and " *edificatione* " among the inhabitants and for the reduction of the disobedient. To strengthen his hand two of his sons received grants of the neighbouring lands of Glenmoriston and Corriemony. The Lairds of Grant, however, were by no means always successful. James, fourth Laird of Freuchie, had helped the Earl of Huntly in a punitive expedition against Lochiel, Clanranald and Glengarry, and, in retribution, Glenurquhart and Glenmoriston were raided in 1544 ; cattle, foodstuffs, household furnishings, everything being carried off, down to the locks and stanchions of Urquhart Castle. In compensation Grant received from Queen Mary, a Charter for large tracts of land belonging to Lochiel and Glengarry. He was, however, unable to collect his rents there or to occupy the land. Successive Lairds could only turn these lands to account by offering a legal title to them to their *de facto* owners in return for the promise of immunity from further raids.

The Lairds of Freuchie secured due feudal rights as barons of their various estates but they rapidly became something more. The first mention of "lye Clan of Grantes" occurred in 1537 in an agreement for the ending of a feud with the Farquharsons, but the son of Bigla had probably begun to build up a clan. By the end of the sixteenth century the Laird of Freuchie was being styled Laird of Grant or Grant of that Ilk.

The process was far more rapid than would have been possible by the natural increase of one family. Patronymics were generally used in the Highlands, but it became customary for the tenants or followers of a chief to take his surname and identify themselves with his family. This was so with Clan Grant. In a list of the parishioners of Duthil in 1527, all the names are Gaelic patronymics. In a second list, dated 1569, there are forty-seven names, all Grant. In a document of 1537, the tenant of Gartenbeg is named John McConquhy. His son in an endorsement of 1581, gives his name as Grant. By the eighteenth century the man-power of the clan was estimated at 850.

On his side the Laird became knit to his people by closer than feudal ties, and in the case of the Grants these bonds between the chief and his clansmen not only were still strong at the time of the '45, but largely survived into the nineteenth century. In the wild days of the sixteenth century the chief was the defender and leader of his clansmen. He held the land that they occupied (in the case of the Grants by legal title, in that of many clans at this time by plain force). He made provision for the widows and children of men who fell in his service and long continued to fulfil this obligation. He represented his clansmen in appeals to the authorities for redress, as for instance in two great raids on Glenurquhart and Glenmoriston and on many lesser occasions. He constantly took up their cause when they were wronged by neighbouring clans, and if they were the aggressors arranged for compensation and prevented the spread of blood feuds. An amusing example happened rather later. Some of Lochiel's men had been raiding in the Laigh land of Moray and had attacked a Grant living there. The Laird of Grant wrote to Lochiel expostulating and demanding compensation. He received a letter of apology for the " misfortunate accident," which had happened because Grant's clansman was living outside his bounds in " Murray land where all men taken their prey," and the raiders did not know that he was a Grant. Lochiel ruefully says that he has had the worst of the affair for eight of his men were dead and over a dozen still under cure, but he suggests that the matter should be " referred to the sight of mutual friends." Under a Charter of 1535, the Laird of Freuchie had very full feudal rights of jurisdiction, and regular Courts were held in Strathspey and Glenurquhart. There are, however, many instances of the Laird's exercise of judicial powers quite outside the law. For instance, the sixth Laird in 1622 declared that it was a disgrace to themselves and their chief that some of his people had gone to law in Edinburgh about a quarrel. He, himself, settled the dispute at once and sent them home. The Laird was of economic importance to his people. In the sixteenth century both the Lairds and the lesser folk mainly lived by raising cattle which had to be sent to Lowland markets, and only a man of some substance could arrange for the sending of the large droves in which beasts were driven and for their protection. In later times, he provided capital for agricultural improvements and gave employment in many other ways. In times of scarcity, right down to the nineteenth century, he imported seed-corn and foodstuffs for his people. Above all, the chief was the focus of his clansmens' lives.

He maintained pipers in Strathspey and Glenurquhart. He and his family gave the lead in social activities. Their weddings and above all their funerals were great events. He exercised boundless hospitality, keeping up the tradition through varying manners and customs, from the feast in the great hall where the Laird sat at his *hie burd* and his retainers occupied trestle tables, to the banquets of the early nineteenth century when every jack-man about the place was crammed into livery to wait on the multitude of guests. In Castle Grant there are early eighteenth-century pictures of some of the retainers of the Chief, his Champion, his piper, and even the Castle henwife (dated 1706), and also of about thirty of the heads of the leading cadet families. Such portraits are unique in a Chief's castle and are a tangible proof of the close bonds that had united Clan Grant for centuries.

The Lairds of Grant, like most other chiefs of clans, down to the seventeenth century provided for their younger sons by granting them portions of their estates, and thus founded cadet branches. On succeeding, such chieftains gave a " bond of manrent " to their chief and in peace and war they acted as his lieutenants. Almost invariably they were his devoted supporters. For instance, in 1584, John (the Gentle) the fourth Laird was old and within a few months of his death. He had lost his eldest son and his authority was evidently slipping. He wrote to " his maist speciall freindis and kynnis men " complaining of his feeble health and that he was " mishandlet " by his neighbours. He was sending his surviving son and grandson to them, desiring to know if they had any fault to find with him so that it might be amended. The very day the letter was received the gentlemen of the Clan gathered in the Church of Cromdale, and replied to it, unanimously declaring that they found no fault with their

"Chief and maister" and that they would support him against all invaders not only with their goods but with their lives.

Two of the most ancient cadet branches were: (a) the first family of Ballindalloch, descended from the eldest son of the first Laird, who owned the land so early as 1520. They founded the families of Dalvey and Dunlugas; and (b) the Grants of Tullochgorm, traditionally descended either from the first Laird's younger brother or from a son of the second Laird. Two other sons of the second Laird (who himself received a charter for Glenurquhart) got Crown charters for Corriemony and for Glenmoriston. From the Corriemony branch is descended the family of Sheuglie and from the Grants of Glenmoriston the family of Carron. Two sons of the third Laird founded the first family of Elchies and the Grants of Ballintomb, who eventually became the Grants of Monymusk in Aberdeenshire. The younger sons of the fourth Laird founded (a) the important family of Rothiemurchus, from whom the second family of Ballindalloch are descended, and (b) the Grants of Moyness and of Lurg. The Grants of Kinchurdie, Gellovie and Gartenbeg are descended from the sixth Laird, and the son of the seventh founded the second family of Elchies.

These branches fared very differently. Some died out comparatively soon. Three—Corriemony (who afterwards held of the chief), Glenmoriston and Rothiemurchus—got Crown charters. Many got heritable possession of their land, while others only held by a lease or, by the seventeenth century, by a wadset (the old Scots form of a mortgage which gave the creditor the use of the land and was a very usual way of providing for younger sons in the Highlands). Two of them—Rothiemurchus and Glenmoriston—achieved a great degree of independence. Though not entirely divided from the main clan, their position is exceptional and requires a separate note (see p. 28).

In the earlier days of Clan Grant, during the sixteenth and seventeenth centuries, the most troublesome and probably the most powerful cadet branch was that of the first family of Ballindalloch. They were a continual thorn in the side of the chief. One early story about them gives interesting side-lights on Highland life of the period. In 1586, a kinsman of Grant of Ballindalloch died, and his widow, who had been a Gordon, quarrelled with young Ballindalloch's uncle who was administering his estate, turned for help to her own kinsmen and married one of them. The uncle, " grudging that any of the surname of Gordon should dwell among them," picked a quarrel and killed one of the Gordon's servants. The Gordon kinsmen then appealed to their chief, the Earl of Huntly, to pursue the slayer by virtue of his office of Sheriff of Inverness-shire. Huntly got a royal commission, and took and burnt the house of Ballindalloch. The Laird of Grant was furious because the death of an ordinary clansman was generally compensated for by a payment of money or cattle. He called on his friends for help, and, within four days, a bond of mutual support was signed by the Earls of Moray and of Athole, Campbell of Cawdor and Lovat, besides some of his leading clansmen. Mackintosh quickly joined the association, and there was raiding and counter-raiding " with far greitair vigour nor it war with forreign enemyis," Huntly being supported by Lochiel and Clanranald, and Grant by the MacGregors. Eventually the Earl of Angus had to be sent north to make peace.

This story brings in the relations between the Laird of Grant and his most powerful neighbours. Strathspey lay between the spheres of influence of the Earls of Moray and of Huntly. The earldom of Moray had passed through many hands and the Earl could only assert himself from time to time, whereas Huntly well deserved his title of the Cock o' the North, and was constantly entrusted, as the Lieutenant of the King, with enforcing the royal authority. His power, however, largely depended on the support given him by his Highland vassals and was by no means absolute. Until almost the end of the sixteenth century successive Lairds of Grant generally kept on excellent terms with the Earls of Huntly. Bonds of maintenance and of manrent were constantly renewed between them. Nevertheless, although they owed Huntly service, the prudent Lairds of Grant did not allow themselves to become embroiled with Moray (Huntly's rival) nor with their closest neighbours, the Chiefs of Clan Mackintosh, who were frequently on bad terms with both Huntly and Moray.

Raiding was endemic. The best-known yarn about it (probably dating, if it really happened at all, from the time of the third Laird) narrates that in punishment for a murder (details vary) Huntly and Grant invaded Deeside. A good many inhabitants were killed in the fighting, and Huntly took their orphaned children back with him to Strathbogie. Some time afterwards Grant visited him there, and, as an amusing sight, was shown the orphans " lobbing " at a long trough into which the broken meats of the castle were thrown. Grant was shocked, and, saying that as he had helped to kill the fathers it was fair that he should assist in maintaining the children, he took all the orphans who were on one side of the trough back with him to Strathspey. They were properly brought up and took the name of Grant, but their descendants were for long known as " The Race of the Trough."

In spite of the wildness of the times the Lairds of Grant in the sixteenth century were already men of considerable substance. Besides their growing estates they had very large herds of cattle and horses and they stored considerable quantities of grain. Even their outlying stronghold of Castle Urquhart at the mouth of that Strath was stocked with feather beds, napery, pots, pans and pewter vessels, besides a kist containing money. All this we know from the melancholy complaints of raids by Camerons and Macdonalds. From family papers we know that the Lairds' personal belongings were considerable. The fourth Laird, who died in 1584, left 30,000 merks in specie and his clothes and armour were valued at £666. Among other things he had a golden chain weighing 20 ounces and a cloak of " French black," " fair lappet " with black velvet worth £60. Such garments would probably be reserved for ceremonial visits to Edinburgh, for a hundred years later accounts show that Ludovick, the eighth Laird, and his man were wearing tartan trews. Among the leading clansmen, we know that Duncan Grant of Rothiemurchus (who died early in the seventeenth century) had two silver cups, but this was evidently rather remarkable for he was known as Duncan of the Cups.

About the middle of the sixteenth century the stirring events in the national history affected the Grants. John, fourth Laird, was in the Palace of Holyrood House when Rizzio was murdered and was one of the courtiers who tried to rescue Queen Mary. Although he was a supporter of the Reformed religion, he was active in helping the Queen until her flight into England. He then made submission to the Regent Moray. In his time the old friendship with Huntly cooled and the estrangement increased as Huntly became involved in plots for the restoration of the Old Faith. In the pitched battle between Huntly and Argyll on the Braes of Glenlivat (in 1594) the Grants fought on Argyll's side.

By the end of the sixteenth and beginning of the

seventeenth century two causes of continual friction with the authorities began to vex the Chiefs of Grant. During the sixteenth century, the authority of the chiefs of clans proved more and more effective while that of the Government was only felt spasmodically, and so the authorities tried to make the chiefs responsible for the conduct of their followers. In 1590, all chiefs and captains of clans were obliged to sign a " General Band " accepting responsibility under heavy cautions. The Laird of Grant had to find one for £10,000. The provisions of the General Band were again and again renewed during the seventeenth and eighteenth centuries and successive Chiefs of Grant were to get into constant trouble upon this account. Discipline within the clan was evidently less strict than within clans less securely established, so that there were unruly elements, while the rich coastal lands of Moray were just beyond the Grant estates and were a sore temptation to clansmen and to undesirable incomers. Among the latter were many of the unfortunate MacGregors.

The early seventeenth century saw the intensification of the persecution of the MacGregors. Deprived of their land, they were forbidden to carry arms and their name was proscribed. The heavy fines levied on anyone who " reset " a MacGregor became a valuable source of revenue to the King and to Argyll, who had the lucrative office of collecting the fines, of which he kept a percentage. The Lairds of Grant were given many commissions to hunt down members of the unfortunate clan but did as little as they possibly could. They and their clansmen were constantly admonished by the Privy Council for harbouring MacGregors, and there are many stories of how they did so. There are several versions of a tale that Grant of Tullochgorm was very fond of the fiddle and much enjoyed the playing of a fugitive MacGregor, in one version named Iain Dubh Ciar (Dusky Black John), who came to his house. His daughter and the young man fell in love with each other. One day, when all her family had gone to market, a party of men who had been sent to capture Iain Dubh Ciar surprised the young pair in the barn. MacGregor plied his sword and the girl stood back to back with him and kept off his assailants with his dirk till all of them were killed. Then the young couple danced together in their joy and Iain Dubh improvised the tune which is now known as the Reel of Tulloch.

It is a matter of sober history that in 1614, the Laird of Grant was ordered to pay 40,000 merks as fines levied on himself and his clansmen (of whom a long list is given) for resetting MacGregors, and that he managed to compound for 16,000 merks. A year earlier Grant of Rothiemurchus had been fined 2,000 merks and Grant of Grant had acted as cautioner for him. The long and special connection of the Grants of Rothiemurchus and the MacGregors, however, is best told in the notes upon that branch. The MacGregors found help not only in Strathspey but in Glenurquhart, where they were said to have had a bad influence on the people, encouraging them in reiving ways. They were, in fact, an element of disturbance in Clan affairs. In their desperate need they were ready to support the quarrel of anyone who would befriend them.

Unfortunately, there was a serious quarrel within Clan Grant in the seventeenth century. Grant of Ballindalloch was already at bitter feud with Grant of Carron, who was the younger son of the first Grant of Glenmoriston and the uncle of the young heir. Ballindalloch had claimed Glenmoriston, declaring that the heir, Carron's young nephew, was illegitimate. Carron had taken up his cause and there had been a series of murderous reprisals on both sides. The Laird of Grant tried to arrange compensation, but Ballindalloch was irreconcilable and in the early seventeenth century was constantly petitioning the Privy Council to bring Seumas an Tuim, the leading man in the Carron family, to justice. The Laird of Grant was much badgered by the Privy Council to capture him. Finally, he was caught, after a desperate struggle, by some outlawed Mackintoshes, who hoped thereby to gain their own pardon. He was warded in Edinburgh Castle, but escaped by means of a rope smuggled in to him in a keg of butter. Ballindalloch employed a band of outlawed MacGregors to catch him. But Seumas an Tuim killed their leader, and, capturing Ballindalloch, kept him prisoner in a disused lime-kiln for twenty-one days before he managed to escape. A price was put on Seumas' head and the Laird of Grant employed fourteen men to hunt him down. In spite of this the Laird was summoned to Edinburgh to answer for his failure and put in ward, although he was in bad health at the time and died (in 1637) immediately after his release. Seumas an Tuim escaped, and gained the patronage of Huntly who procured a pardon for him; and he was employed by his lordship in hunting MacGregors and Covenanters.

From the middle of the seventeenth century many of the Highland clans engaged in the various Risings on behalf of the House of Stuart. The Lairds of Grant were consistently opposed to them. In the Civil War the seventh Laird supported the Covenant (not very vigorously), and he and his tenants suffered severely when Montrose and his army occupied Strathspey. Eventually, Grant had to make submission to the Marquis, and, in consequence, he and his people suffered equally severely from the Covenanting army after Montrose left the country. Nevertheless, when Charles II was recognised as the Covenanted King of Scotland and the Scots

Parliament called out the man-power of the country to support him, a contingent of seven-score men from the Clan, led by the Chief's brother, joined the Scots army in 1651, and fought for the King at Worcester.

The eighth Laird sat in that momentous Scots Parliament of 1689, that offered the Crown to William and Mary, and he and his clansmen co-operated with General Mackay in the series of feints and counter-marches in Strathspey, between the armies of Major-General Mackay and Viscount Dundee, before the battle of Killiecrankie. On the other hand, Glenmoriston supported Dundee and fought for King James. His son "from a hunter became a warrior" and at the head of his father's men greatly distinguished himself at Killiecrankie. After Dundee's death the Jacobite forces were inefficiently led. Their final defeat took place in Strathspey at the battle of the Haughs of Cromdale (1690). They were taken by surprise by an attack by the Government forces in which three hundred Grants took an important part. This contingent afterwards helped to garrison Fort William.

In the time of the Jacobite Rising of 1715, the old Laird had given the control of the estates and the Clan to his eldest son, Brigadier Alexander Grant, who had served under Marlborough and was appointed Governor of Edinburgh Castle. A younger brother, George, was in command of a body of Grants equipped and maintained by the Brigadier and officered by the gentlemen of the Clan (see p. 25). It was vitally important to prevent the Jacobites from mastering the Northern Highlands, and John Forbes of Culloden and Lord Lovat (then strongly pro-Hanoverian) hurried north. Forbes made his influence felt and Lovat brought his clan over to the Government side. George Grant and his men played a most important part in supporting them and in regaining the town of Inverness from the Jacobites. Grant of Glenmoriston, on the other hand, supported the Jacobite cause. His estate was forfeited, but it was a poor bargain for the Government. Rents were paid to the old owner or not at all, and the Laird of Grant eventually, acting on behalf of Glenmoriston, was able to buy back the estate for the nominal sum of £1,086.

Although the Lairds of Grant had supported the successful side, their losses and expenses had been heavy. These were estimated at £12,540 for Dundee's campaign, and £20,000 in the '15; and no compensation had been given.

At the time of the '45 the Chief of Clan Grant was Sir James (first Baronet), who was a member of Parliament and lived mostly in London. His son, Ludovick, was in charge of the estates. Besides the ingratitude of the Government there were reasons why the Chief and his son were not enthusiastic supporters of the Hanoverians. Though both were Whigs, Grant and Duncan Forbes of Culloden were political rivals, and Grant and his son disagreed with Duncan Forbes' policy of raising Independent Companies. They urged that, as was so successfully done in the Jacobite army, the whole man-power of the clans whose Chiefs were loyal to the House of Hanover should be called out to serve under their own Chiefs. No doubt the cheese-paring financial policy of the Government was one reason against the adoption of the Grants' plan, but Duncan Forbes of Culloden used the gift of the commissions in the Independent Companies as an inducement to secure the loyalty of clans of which he was doubtful, and both the Chief and the gentlemen of the Clan did not consider that the Grants had received their fair share. Sir James advised Ludovick " to stay at home and take care of his country and join no party." Ludovick, as a matter of fact, made several offers of help to the Lord President Forbes and General Loudon, the Hanoverian leaders at Inverness, which were all turned down, and several times he called out the Clan and protected his own estates and those of his neighbours; and he was unremitting in his efforts to prevent his clansmen from disobeying his orders and going to join the Prince. The majority of the clan in Strathspey were half-hearted when ordered to support the Government— many of them had Jacobite sympathies, which probably explains why the Grant Independent Company proved so ineffective and surrendered Inverness Castle to the Jacobites.

In marked contrast was the zeal of those clansmen who served the Prince. Grants from Glenmoriston were among the earliest to join him; and when young Glenmoriston, in his haste to bring up reinforcements in time for the fight with Cope, entered the Prince's presence travel-stained and unshaven, and was reproached for his appearance, he burst out: "It is not beardless boys who will do your Highness's turn." The Grants of Sheuglie and Corriemony and many others defied the anger of the Laird of Grant, who was not only their chief but the owner of whom they held their land. Traditions clustered thickly about a young clansman, Colquhoun Grant, the son of Grant of Burnside, who served in the Prince's bodyguard throughout the campaign. One of the tales about him is that, single-handed and on foot, he chased a party of dragoons after the rout at Prestonpans to Edinburgh Castle, and, when the gates were shut in his teeth behind the fugitives, he stuck his dirk into the wood in defiance. Successive Lairds of Rothiemurchus had given asylum to leading Jacobite fugitives after the Rising of the '15 and Glenshiel (1719), and once more did so in the dreadful aftermath of Culloden. The Prince gave the brother of Tullochgorm a portrait and a fishing rod in recognition of his services.

Ludovick Grant, the acting chief, was the least worthy member of his long line. After Culloden he was active in hunting down fugitives, and he received the voluntary surrender of sixteen men of Glenurquhart and sixty-eight of Glenmoriston, and handed them over unconditionally to Cumberland. It was universally believed in the two glens that the men, whom he had already failed to capture, had been given some assurance before they surrendered. But they were shipped to London, and then, without trial, sent to Barbados. By 1749, only eighteen had survived the brutal treatment they had met with, and only seven or eight were able eventually to return home. The Laird of Grant's losses and expenses in the '45 were estimated at £20,000, for which he received no compensation.

Parliamentary elections aroused intense excitement in the North during the eighteenth century. From the end of the seventeenth century seven members of the family of Grant of Grant sat successively in Parliament. Members of the family played a prominent part in offering the Crown to William and Mary, and in the negotiations that led to the Act of Union, but they made little mark in the English House of Commons. The long sequence of representation during the eighteenth century is, however, a striking tribute to the influence of the Lairds of Grant. The franchise was limited to men holding land directly of the King or with a high property qualification, and in 1734, the total number of voters in Inverness-shire was only sixteen. For a large part of the century there were no party contests as we know them, and the struggle was between two branches of the Whigs whose differences lay mainly in the personalities of their leaders. In the actual electoral contests, also, personality, influence and family connections were the main considerations, and, in the Highlands, clan loyalties played a great part. The electoral campaigns were keenly fought and feeling ran high. For instance, in 1733 John Forbes of Culloden, supported by his brother Duncan and MacLeod of

MacLeod, wished to contest Inverness-shire. A doggerel poem recorded that :

> Tho' the Brothers did brag at last they did fag,
> Notwithstanding two clans was their shield.
> For the sight of a Grant made all their hearts pant,
> That they durst not appear in the field.

The most interesting political contest took place so late as 1820. The Chief (he had succeeded to the earldom of Seafield) was an invalid and was living with his sisters at Grant Lodge, Elgin. His brother, Colonel Francis William Grant, was standing as a Tory for the " Elgin Burghs " (five north-eastern burghs at that time forming a joint-constituency). His Whig opponent was Colonel Duff, a brother of the Earl of Fife. Most of the people of Elgin were violently pro-Fife. Known opponents were ejected from the burgh and they barricaded the gates of Grant Lodge, letting no one in or out. However, Lady Anne, the sister of the Chief, managed to smuggle messages out to Grant of Congash (the Strathspey factor) and to a lad of fifteen of the family of Tullechgorm (afterwards Field-Marshal Sir Patrick Grant). To the latter she wrote that, boy as he was, she knew he would not tamely allow his Chief and his sisters to be insulted. Immediately the Fiery Cross was sent round and within a few hours 800 men had gathered and set out for Elgin under the command of the gentlemen of the Clan. They sang as they marched, but as it was Sunday they stuck to psalm tunes till after midnight. The townspeople barricading Grant Lodge fled at their coming and their Chief and Lady Anne came out to welcome and thank them. The authorities of Elgin promised that there should be no further molestation, and the men marched home without doing any damage whatever to the town.[1]

[1] The story of the Raid was written down by Sir Patrick Grant, the grandfather of the present writer.

The Elgin Raid was the last occasion on which a clan was raised by the Fiery Cross. It shows how strongly the spirit of clanship had survived among the Grants. In the preceding century we have interesting evidence of the wearing of a clan tartan. About 1703, the tenants of the Laird of Grant were ordered to wear " short coates, trewes, and short hose of red and green set dyce all braid springed betwixt " when summoned to attend the Laird for hosting or hunting, and in 1710, according to a MS. history of the Clan, the clansmen were ordered to gather at the usual meeting-place wearing plaids of red and green. The Chief met them there and told them that because of age and infirmity he could no longer lead them and that therefore he was handing over the command of the Clan to his son Alexander. Then, turning to his son, he said that that day he made him " a very great present "—the command of the Clan—and urged him to use the clansmen well. It was this son, who, in the '15, raised the body of Grants commanded by his brother (see p. 20). They were described as wearing " ane livery of tartan." Not only did he equip and maintain them but, in the old tradition, he took responsibility for the widows and orphans of those who might fall.

After the '45, when in so many clans the ties that bound chiefs and clansmen together were weakening, the Grants were particularly fortunate in being ruled by " good Sir James " (3rd Baronet). (He took over control in 1761, succeeded in 1771 and died in 1808.) He reorganised his estates in the interests of the lesser tenants. Neither in his time nor in those of his successors was there any " clearing " of the tenantry on the Grant estates. On the contrary, he did everything he could to keep his people from emigrating.

One of his plans was the founding of Grant-town in 1766. There had been several attempts to establish a village and market close to Castle Grant, but it was Sir James who planned the town and laid it out as we know it. In the days before factories several handicraft industries were flourishing in many parts of Scotland. In Strathspey itself there was a lumbering industry on a considerable scale, the pine logs from the great natural forests being floated down the Spey to the sea at Garmouth, and with the great improvements in agriculture that Sir James was encouraging there was a growing demand for local craftsmen. Sir James hoped that a small industrial community would grow up and would keep the people from emigrating. With this objective he also founded the village of Lewiston in Glenurquhart. During the terrible famine of 1782, he imported food to maintain his people. When Revolutionary France declared war on Britain in 1793, he was one of the first of the Highland Lairds to raise both a "fencible" and a regular regiment (the 97th or Strathspey Regiment) within his clan.

It is our good fortune that vivid descriptions of life in Strathspey about the end of his reign survive in the inimitable *Memoirs of a Highland Lady* by Elizabeth Grant of Rothiemurchus (Mrs. Smith of Baltiboys). The farms were largely occupied by gentlemen farmers on long leases, commonly known as tacksmen. Many of them had served in the Army in their youth and their younger sons went far afield wherever the expanding possessions of Britain had use for their services. They had breeding that enabled them to mingle with their richer kinsfolk, the Lairds, and the simplicity of folk living on the land. Gaelic was their mother tongue and they were nurtured in the traditions of Gaeldom. The ancient culture of the race was common to gentle and simple alike. What Mrs. Grant of Laggan wrote of Badenoch—the upper reaches of the Strath—was no doubt also true of farther down—in every home there was a musician and a poet in every hamlet.

Although the pine forests of Strathspey have existed from time immemorial, the great plantings that give the district such a distinctive character, even after the fellings of two world wars, were begun by the second son of Good Sir James, Francis William (the successful candidate in the 1820 election), who succeeded his elder brother. By 1837, he had planted $31\frac{1}{2}$ million trees.

The way in which the titles borne by the Chiefs of Grant came into the family is rather complicated. The Baronetcy had been granted to the Colquhouns of Luss, but the only child of Sir Humphry Colquhoun married James Grant, brother of the Laird of Grant, and Sir Humphry in 1704 obtained a new patent enabling his son-in-law to succeed to the baronetcy. This James Grant eventually succeeded his brother as Laird of Grant.

The Earldom of Seafield is a Scots peerage. Sir Ludovick Grant of Grant had married Lady Margaret Ogilvie, daughter of the Earl of Findlater and Seafield, in 1735. The male Ogilvie line died out, and as the Seafield title (but not the Findlater) can be inherited by heirs general, i.e., by a woman, her grandson (who was already Laird of Grant) in 1811, succeeded to the Earldom of Seafield with its great estates.

More than once there had been suggestions that the Laird of Grant should himself be granted a peerage (the retort " Then wha'll be Laird o' Grant ? " is attributed to several chiefs), but it was not till 1855 that John Charles (the son of Francis William, the great planter) was created Baron Strathspey in the Peerage of Great Britain. This title descends in the male line, and, as his grandson left an only daughter, who succeeded her father as Countess of Seafield, the Barony and the Chiefship went to her uncle and his heirs.

The Grants of Glenmoriston and of Rothiemurchus

The Grants of Glenmoriston and Rothiemurchus have constantly been alluded to in the general history of the Clan. There is a most romantic (and unlikely) tradition about the origin of John Mor, son of the second Laird of Freuchie, who got a charter for Glenmoriston. His father, known as the Red Bard, is said to have gone to a great hunt given by the Laird of Kincardine in Glenmore. There were festivities afterwards, and the daughter of the Laird of Kincardine in course of time bore the Red Bard a son. The appearance of a ball of fire in the Laird of Kincardine's cattleyard foretold that the boy would be remarkable, and remarkable he was for size and strength. He fought and vanquished an English champion whose feats of strength had put all the men of Edinburgh to shame, and the Town Council bade him name his reward. He asked for what he could carry out of Edinburgh Castle. His father was a prisoner there so he took him on his back. The Laird of Mackintosh was also in ward, so he took him on his back as well and carried the two men out. In reward his father gave him the lands of Glenmoriston, and the Laird of Mackintosh bade nine of his men lie down in the burn at Moy so that Iain Mor should walk over dry-shod. As a matter of fact, the name of Iain Mor's mother is unknown, and it was from the King that Iain Mor got his charter in 1509, and, so far from being in Ward, his father was then in high favour. The Laird of Mackintosh *was* actually a prisoner about that time.

Iain Mor was certainly of outstanding ability, and he acquired land in Strathspey (which he gave to a younger son, the ancestor of the Grants of Carron), and also about Inverness, including the barony of Culcabock. The family's exploits in the cause of the Stuarts have been alluded to, but the story of how the Grants of Glenmoriston lost Culcabock but saved Glenmoriston deserves to be told. The family had got into debt to a neighbouring laird, Robertson of Inches, who took legal proceedings, and in 1645, the occupation of the lands of Culcabock and Glenmoriston was granted to him, and he was to retain permanent possession if Glenmoriston did not redeem them within a given time. Robertson was able to occupy Culcabock, although the kinsmen of Glenmoriston (the Laird was a minor at the time) raided his lands in retaliation. In 1662, Glenmoriston, who had come of age, offered to resign his claims to Culcabock, if Robertson would pay him 8,000 merks and give up all claim to Glenmoriston. Robertson refused, and on New Year's night the citizens of Inverness were aroused by the burning of the barns of Culcabock. It was easily guessed who had instigated the deed. In March the stacks also were burnt, but Robertson still refused to compound. Glenmoriston then arranged a meeting in Inverness itself between himself, Robertson, and the Lairds of Brodie and of Culloden. No compromise was reached, and when the meeting broke up Glenmoriston called out sixteen men whom he had hidden close by, seized Robertson and carried him off to Glenmoriston. There Robertson was induced to promise to pay Glenmoriston

THE CLAN GRANT

7,000 merks. The Privy Council, however, had ordered the Earl of Moray, as Sheriff of Inverness, to arrest Glenmoriston. He was captured, escaped, but was again captured by the Robertsons of Struan. He was released on bail, and, in 1666, a settlement was reached. Glenmoriston acknowledged Robertson's right to Culcabock, and Robertson gave up all claims to Glenmoriston.

The family of Rothiemurchus is descended from Patrick, son of the fourth Laird of Grant. He received a charter for Rothiemurchus from his father about 1570. The district had long been occupied by the Shaws, a branch of the Mackintoshes; they had sold it in 1539 to Huntly, from whom the Laird of Grant had bought it in 1567. The Chief of the Mackintoshes was most anxious to get it back, and he and his Shaw kinsfolk "inquietit" the Grants in the occupation of their new possession. The struggle for Rothiemurchus between the Shaws, whose chief still had land in Strathspey and lived at Dalnavert, and the descendants of Patrick Grant continued for two generations. Finally, according to tradition, James (the grandson of Patrick) killed the Chief of the Shaws. His kindred buried the dead Shaw with his forebears in Rothiemurchus churchyard, but next morning his widow found her husband's body propped up against her door. The reburial and raising of the corpse took place several times, but Shaw was finally buried in the church under the Laird's own seat, who is said to have stamped on his grave whenever he entered the church. This Laird of Rothiemurchus' son was Patrick MacAlpine, probably the most outstanding man of his line. He obtained a Crown Charter for the lands of Rothiemurchus. He gained the name MacAlpine because he had been formally adopted into Clan Gregor on account of his good offices to that clan. He was on good terms with Rob Roy, and, relying on his promise of help, he took a very high line with Mackintosh in a dispute that had arisen between them over a mill. Mackintosh prepared to invade Rothiemurchus; and as MacAlpine was on bad terms with his own chief, and alone was no match for the Mackintoshes and other members of Clan Chattan, he became very uneasy. As he brooded, someone laid a hand on his shoulder and said: "What though the purse be empty to-night, who knows how full it may be in the morn?" It was Rob Roy, but alone. MacAlpine asked where his men were, and Rob Roy called for his piper. The piper marched up and down in front of the house playing the MacGregors' Gathering, and, as he played, by twos and threes Rob Roy's band gathered by the river till 150 were there, and by then the piper was fit to burst. But as they had come, the Mackintoshes had stolen away by threes and fours till none was left. Rob Roy wrote to Mackintosh threatening dire reprisals if MacAlpine was molested.[1]

Patrick MacAlpine's younger brother, William, married a daughter of the Laird of Grant in 1711; and about the same time he bought the estate of Ballindalloch from the representative of the old branch, who had got into financial difficulties. He founded a new family of Grants of Ballindalloch.

---

[1] This story is told by Mrs. Smith (Miss Elizabeth Grant of Rothiemurchus) in her *Memoirs of a Highland Lady*.

Grant Pipe Tunes

I should like to thank Colonel J. P. Grant of Rothiemurchus for his kindness in supplying the following list of tunes and the comments upon them.

PIOBAIREACHD	.. ..	Craigellachie, or the Grants' Gathering.
MARCHES	.. .. ..	Captain Grant.
		The Braes of Castle Grant.
STRATHSPEYS	.. ..	The Rothiemurchus Rant.
		Tullochgorm (originally a fiddle tune).
		Monymusk (originally a fiddle tune).
REELS	.. .. ..	The Reel of Tulloch.
		The Burning of the Black Mill.
JIG	.. ..	Braeriach (modern).

Frontispiece

Portrait of Alasdair Mor Grant, The Laird's Champion. Painted in 1714 by Waitt. A boat is shown in the background, and he is said to have been the Laird's ferryman, and, in his youth, to have walked to London with his Curragh on his back. When he launched it on the Thames the onlookers threw gold pieces into it, which Alasdair presented to his chief asking him to buy Lady Grant a few pins with the money.

Badge

Scots Fir (*Pinus Sylvestris*).

"The Grants of Strath Spey, . . .
That's the band not scanty, that
Would put pine to the flagpole" . . .

From a poem by Iain Lom (1620?–1716?). Translated by Hugh MacDiarmid in "The Golden Treasury of Scottish Poetry." (Macmillan, 1948.)

Grant Clan Names

Gilroy, MacGilroy, Macilroy.

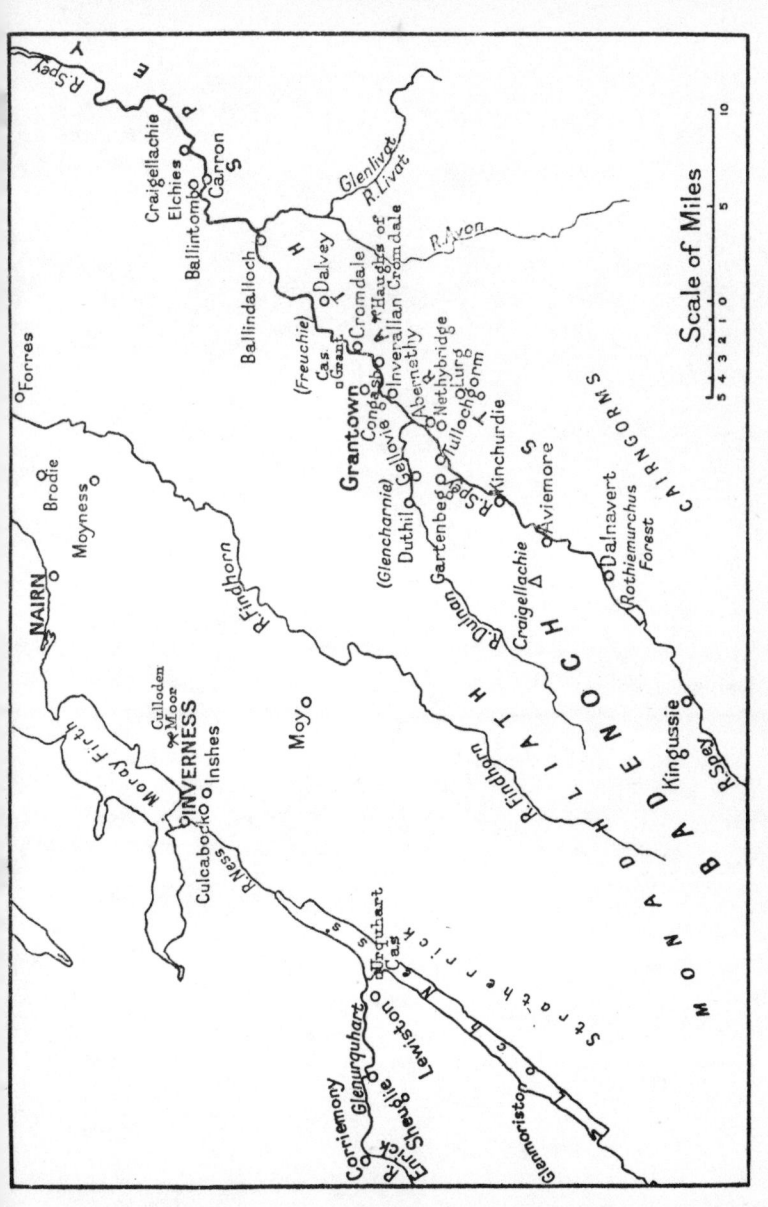